KT-558-535

C152020662

KENT
ARTS & LIBRARIES

C152020662

20TH CENTURY fashion

THE **80S** & **90S**

POWER DRESSING *to* SPORTSWEAR

20TH CENTURY FASHION – THE '80s & '90s
was produced by

David West ÅÅ Children's Books
7 Princeton Court
55 Felsham Road
London SW15 1AZ

Picture Research: Carlotta Cooper/Brooks Krikler
Research
Editor: Clare Oliver
Consultant: Helen Reynolds

First published in Great Britain in 1999 by
Heinemann Library, Halley Court, Jordan Hill,
Oxford OX2 8EJ, a division of Reed Educational and
Professional Publishing Limited.

OXFORD MELBOURNE AUCKLAND
JOHANNESBURG BLANTYRE GABORONE
IBADAN PORTSMOUTH (NH) USA CHICAGO

Copyright © 1999 David West Children's Books

All rights reserved. No part of this publication may be
reproduced, stored in a retrieval system, or
transmitted in any form or by any means, electronic,
mechanical, photocopying, recording, or otherwise
without either prior written permission of the
Publishers or a licence permitting restricted copying in
the United Kingdom issued by the Copyright
Licensing Agency Ltd., 90 Tottenham Court Road,
London W1P 0LP.

ISBN 0 431 09553 1 (HB)   ISBN 0 431 09560 4 (PB)
03 02   03 02
10 9 8 7 6 5 4 3   10 9 8 7 6 5 4 3 2

British Library Cataloguing in Publication Data

Lomas, Clare
Power dressing to sportswear (1980s-1990s). -
(Fashion in the twentieth century)
1. Fashion - History - 20th century - Juvenile
literature
2. Costume - 20th century - Juvenile literature
I. Title
391'.00904

Printed and bound in Italy.

PHOTO CREDITS :
Abbreviations: t-top, m-middle,
b-bottom, r-right, l-left
Cover tl & pages 3tl, 5br, 10r, 11ml,
12r, 13ml, 15bl: Michel Arnaud ©
Vogue/Condé Nast Publications Ltd;
Cover tm, b.2 & pages 7bl, 24tl,
24br: Kim Knott © Vogue/Condé
Nast Publications Ltd; Cover mr &
pages 3mr, 6br, 21r: Andrew
Macpherson © Vogue/Condé Nast
Publications Ltd; Cover b.1 & pages
6bl, 7tl, 22bl, 22-23, 23tr, 26tr, 27tr:
Arthur Elgort © Vogue/Condé Nast
Publications Ltd; Cover bm & page
29bl: Peter Lindbergh © Vogue/Condé
Nast Publications Ltd; Cover br &
pages 5tr, 6tr, 7mr, 16bl, 20tr, 20bl,
21t, 22tr, 24-25, 25br, 27br: Redferns;
4tl, 8tr, 8-9, 9tr, 9br, 10tl, 10bl, 11br,
13tr, 13br, 14tl, 15br, 16tl, 18tl, 18ml,
18bl, 18-19, 19tr, 22br, 25bl, 27ml,
28br, 29tr: Frank Spooner Pictures;
4-5b, 26tl: Sudhir Pithwa ©
Vogue/Condé Nast Publications Ltd;
5ml, 11mr: Spreckley Pittham; 7br,
14tr, 15tl: Alex Chatelain ©
Vogue/Condé Nast Publications Ltd;
12l: Robert Erdman © Vogue/Condé
Nast Publications Ltd; 14b, 26bl:
Patrick Demarchelier © Vogue/Condé
Nast Publications Ltd; 16m: Albert
Watson © Vogue/Condé Nast
Publications Ltd; 17bl: Steve Landis ©
Vogue/Condé Nast Publications Ltd;
17r: P. Lange © Vogue/Condé Nast
Publications Ltd; 8bl: Michel Haddi ©
Vogue/Condé Nast Publications Ltd;
23br: Tim Geaney © Vogue/Condé
Nast Publications Ltd; 26-27: David
Parfitt © Vogue/Condé Nast
Publications Ltd; 28bl: Tom Munro ©
Vogue/Condé Nast Publications Ltd;
28-29: ICI

With special thanks to the Picture
Library & Syndication Department at
Vogue Magazine/Condé Nast
Publications Ltd.

*An explanation of difficult
words can be found in the
glossary on page 30.*

20TH CENTURY fashion

THE 80s & 90s

POWER DRESSING to SPORTSWEAR

Clare Lomas

Heinemann
LIBRARY

CONTENTS

For successful career women, power dressing was all about projecting an image of businesslike glamour.

After the crash of the stock markets in October '87, a softer, less aggressive look replaced power dressing.

The HIGH-TECH '80s & '90s

The 1980s and '90s was a time of rapid technological advances. The period witnessed the births of the Internet, the CD and satellite television. More than ever before, people were bombarded with information, and cultures and styles cross-fertilized. Politics, too, had an enormous impact.

Rave arrived in the late-'80s and gave fashion a new lease of life. Clothing for clubbing was not confined to the clubs for long.

Economies swung back and forth between recession and boom. There was social unrest, as capitalism took hold and workers lost basic rights.

Youth movements had influenced dress since the 1950s, now it was time for twenty- and thirty-somethings to take centre stage. In the boom of the '80s, yuppies bought into a whole lifestyle with their designer suits and high-tech accessories.

Mobile phones and digital organizers were fashion statements as well as business tools.

When the world stock markets crashed in 1987, the backlash had already begun. Power dressing had had its day. Sheer greed was replaced by a conscience, whether people raised money for AIDS victims or campaigned on 'green' issues, for example the destruction of the rainforests. Designers such as Katharine Hamnett and companies such as the Body Shop turned fashion and beauty products into political statement.

Supermodels became huge celebrities, earning fantastic fees to 'get out of bed' and demanding to travel by Concorde. Superstar designers, under pressure, raided every look, from current sub-cultures to fashions of the past.

Jean-Paul Gaultier created a vogue for underwear as outerwear with his sculpted bustiers and evening gowns.

FROTH & frills

The beginning of the 1980s was a time of high unemployment, especially in Britain, which was experiencing its worst recession for 50 years.

Pop pin-ups Duran Duran wore the foppish bows and floppy haircuts of new romantic style.

Rifat Ozbek created this punky version of the dandy look ('87).

LONG, SHORT OR SHORTER

This uncertainty was reflected in dress. Three different skirt lengths could be worn: a three-quarter-length 'peasant' skirt, gathered at the waist; a slightly shorter pencil skirt; or a flouncy, tiered ra-ra that ended mid-thigh.

FIRST FRILLS

Romantic fashions were one way to escape from the harsh economic problems of the time. Laura Ashley (1925–85), famous for her loose-fitting flowery dresses during the '70s, was a proponent of the new romantic look. She used old-fashioned embroidery techniques such as broderie anglaise, pin-tucking and smocking. Lace was used to trim delicate pinafores worn over layered petticoats.

LAVISH WITH LACE

Lace was central to the new romantic look, while velvet and brocade were used for knickerbockers or waistcoats. Colours were rich – deep maroons or forest greens – in contrast to the bright, white lace shirts with ruffled collars.

Key to the new romantic look were extras, like waistcoats and cummerbunds. Dandy details included ribbon-covered seams on trousers and velvet lapels.

6

This romantic evening gown ('82) was designed by the Emanuels, who made Princess Diana's wedding dress.

In fact, ruffles were added everywhere, from necklines and cuffs to hems. Such frilliness decorated the wedding dress of Lady Diana Spencer when she married Prince Charles in 1981. She wore a fantasy creation of ivory silk taffeta designed by husband-and-wife team David (*b.*1953) and Elizabeth (*b.*1953) Emanuel.

POP STAR DANDIES

Vivienne Westwood (*b.*1941) also helped popularize the romantic look. Her Pirates collection ('81) was worn by pop stars such as Adam Ant, who dressed up in a gold-braided jacket and swashbuckling boots for his *Stand and Deliver* pop video.

BATTY GOTHS

In '81 a new London club, the Batcave, became the birthplace of the goth movement. Recreating the gothic style of the 1800s, goths sought inspiration from novels such as *Dracula* (1897). Fabrics (in black, blood reds and purples) included velvet and lace, mixed with fishnet and leather.

Goth hair, dyed black and backcombed, was teased out to frame a deathly face with severe black eye and lip make-up.

BACK IN TIME

The romantic past did not stop with highwaymen and pirates. Ralph Lauren (*b.*1939) looked to the first settlers for his Prairie, or Frontier, collection. He used layers of striped and checked cotton fabrics, flannel shirts, hooded capes and ruffled blouses for an American version of the nostalgic look.

A plume of ostrich feathers tops this lavish frock-coat in gilded silk brocade ('85).

NEW *man*

As women grew more independent, men lost their traditional role as breadwinner and head of the family. In fact, the family seemed to be in decline as the divorce rate soared and there were more single parents. Men needed to re-invent themselves, and the media was on hand to help.

CITY PEACOCKS

From the beginning of the 1980s, men became more interested in looking good. The suit was the standard city wear, but to stand out this could be jazzed up with showy accessories. In particular, brightly-coloured waistcoats and shirts took off. Designer Paul Smith (*b*.1946), who had launched his first menswear collection in '76, recognised the new market and its spending power. He created shirts in bold prints of fruits or flowers. These were clothes for go-getters who were confident enough to wear 'feminine' colours and patterns.

A small child was the ultimate fashion accessory of the period, especially for the new man.

MAKING UP

Cosmetics companies were anxious to tap this market of style-conscious males. Traditionally, men had only bought aftershave, but now they were encouraged to buy facial balms, scrubs and moisturizers. The Body Shop pioneered a range of toiletries for men. Others followed close behind.

A Moschino patchwork jacket ('88) was worn open to reveal feminine rosettes on a rose-printed shirt.

Jean-Paul Gaultier even sent men down the cat-walk in skirts. Few – besides Gaultier himself – took up the style, but it certainly got plenty of press attention!

CARING & SHARING

Soon the media picked up on this new breed of feminized man and gave him a name: new man. A far cry from traditional, reserved males, new man was understanding and tremblingly sensitive. The most enduring image of him was Athena's poster of a bare-chested man holding a nude baby. With many men losing their jobs in the recession which came at the end of the decade, a few men *did* stay at home looking after the children while their partners went out to work.

In the '80s, Y-fronts bought by your mum or wife were definitely out and Calvin Klein boxers were in.

MEDIA HYPE

Before long there was a backlash: 'laddism'. This described young men who returned to 'old-fashioned values' such as rowdiness, sexism and drinking beer. But did new man or new lad really exist? Both have been dismissed as media hype, whether it was aimed at selling men more clothes, toiletries – or lager! But what cannot be denied is that in the 1990s there was an explosion of new magazines aimed at men, such as *GQ*, *Vogue Homme*, *FHM*, *Maxim* and *Loaded*. All of these sold in large enough numbers to suggest that men really were interested in style.

DESIGNER BABIES

Babies were big sellers in the '80s and '90s. The blockbuster movie *Three Men and A Baby* ('87) captured the mood. It starred Tom Selleck, Steve Guttenberg and Ted Danson as three bachelors who are left to look after a baby girl. Audiences may not have been sure if new man existed, but they enjoyed watching how the men coped in a traditionally female role! In real life too, it became outdated to leave all the nurturing to women and magazines gave tips on how to have an equal relationship.

Tom Cruise (right, with wife Nicole Kidman and their child) threw himself into fatherhood.

POWER *dressing*

Sue Ellen, wife of oilman, JR Ewing in TV's Dallas, *had glamorous clothes and a super-rich lifestyle.*

During the 1980s more and more women were employed in high-powered jobs. Prime minister Margaret Thatcher, who began her career looking like a housewife, soon switched to smart, crisp suits. Power dressing was about being visibly successful in a man's world.

Top designers, such as Valentino (who designed this yellow outfit in '84), Moschino and Karl Lagerfeld at Chanel created expensive clothes to get wealthy women noticed.

A WOMAN'S WORLD

Women needed garments that were businesslike, but elegant. They wore tailored jackets with padded shoulders to emphasize slim hips. Suits came in attention-seeking colours or businesslike pinstripes and were worn with high heels and bright red lipstick.

SOAP STYLE

The glamorous woman who 'had it all' was popular in soap operas at the time: characters included Sue Ellen Ewing (played by Linda Gray) in *Dallas* and Alexis Carrington Colby (Joan Collins) and Krystle Carrington (Linda Evans) in *Dynasty*. Soaps revealed the look for men, too. The stars of *Miami Vice* wore double-breasted designer suits with vests or teeshirts underneath and slip-on Gucci loafers. Their designer stubble emphasized their rugged masculinity – or maybe they were too busy to shave!

Actor Don Johnson (left) shows off the casual look, wearing designer stubble – and no socks!

SELLING A LIFESTYLE

Giorgio Armani (*b*.1934) was the king of the power suit. He introduced diffusion lines – clothing with a designer label but at a more affordable price. He also created the power-dresser's favourite fragrance, 'Giorgio', which was so overpowering that it was banned from some restaurants! Other key lifestyle designers were Ralph Lauren and Calvin Klein (*b*.1942).

TAKING OFF ... SLOWING DOWN

High-street shops such as Next in Britain and Gap in the United States provided designer-style separates to wannabe power-dressers. But the ability to buy a glamorous lifestyle was lost for many following Black Friday in October 1987. As stock markets around the world crashed, millions were wiped off the value of shares and many yuppies lost their money and their jobs.

SHOWING OFF

The yuppie carried a filofax or an electronic organizer such as an Apple Newton, to keep track of essential business meetings. Mobile phones, laptop computers and expensive cars were other important yuppie accessories. The key was to show off your wealth and to look like the executive of a big company – whether you were one or not.

For the male executive, the ultimate in suit chic was an Armani, such as this one in Prince-of-Wales check.

Whether it was a Jaguar, BMW or Porsche, the young professional required transport that was sleek, speedy – and extremely expensive!

GLAMOUR

If the suit was the essential daytime look for the corporate world, in the evening ballgowns came out to play. Once again, fashion was all about competition and the idea was to outdress everyone else! Puffed sleeves and frills were extremely popular, along with sequins, lace, tulle and taffeta.

HAVING A BALL

In 1986 a fashion called the puffball skirt (the skirt literally looking like a puffed-out ball of fabric), was shown on the cat-walk by Christian Lacroix (b.1951). It was similar to Vivienne Westwood's mini-crini (a shorter version of the crinoline dresses of the 1800s). Neither style caught on, but they both caught the extravagant mood of the time.

US designer Oscar de la Renta provided a sleek alternative to full skirts with this elegant evening dress ('85).

GLITZY VERSACE

If money was no object, the most showy designer was Gianni Versace (1946–97). He launched his first collection in '78 and was soon known for his use of extravagant fabrics and trimmings. He used mock animal prints, such as zebra, leopard and crocodile, with soft leathers encrusted with huge fake jewels. It is claimed to have been Versace's sexy dresses that launched the supermodels in the early '90s.

To emphasize the shape of the puffball, it was worn with a tight corset and sculpted bolero.

Never far from the headlines, Versace's designs hit the news in '94, when actress Liz Hurley appeared at a film première clad in a Versace dress of black fabric held together with gold safety pins. Other celebrities who wore Versace included singers Madonna, Prince and Elton John, actress Elizabeth Taylor and Diana, Princess of Wales.

Versace designed also for the theatre and ballet which influenced his ever-dramatic fashion work. This jewelled ballgown is from his Summer '92 collection.

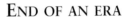

TOUCHES OF GLAMOUR

The House of Chanel once again had a makeover when Karl Lagerfeld (*b.*1938) joined. But the classic quilted handbag with its 'CC' logo and chunky gilt strap remained an essential for wealthy women. For those who were not, fragrances such as Chanel's 'Coco' for women (and 'Egoïste' for men) provided designer glamour at a fraction of the cost. And to finish off those luxurious ballgowns, arms and necks dripped with Rolex watches and Cartier jewels. Diamanté and faux pearl chokers were popular, and even tiaras made a comeback.

For men, a crumpled designer suit, such as this one by Girbaud ('84), was a casual – but reassuringly expensive – alternative to black tie.

END OF AN ERA
The '80s was a period of wealth – for a lucky few, at least. Margaret Thatcher in Britain and Ronald Reagan in the United States were capitalists. They believed you could achieve anything as long as you worked hard enough. To assist this, borrowing money was made easier. High-fliers took out large loans and made millions by buying and selling shares. But in October '87 the stock market crashed. The recession soon spread: estate agents, for example, were hit as people failed to pay their mortgages and house prices fell.

City whizz kids lost fortunes when the stock market crashed.

The JAPANESE look & NEW AGE

For those in search of a more individual look than the power suit, the new breed of Japanese designers who had made their names in the 1970s seemed to have the answer.

Issey Miyake opened his Miyake Design Studio (MDS) in Tokyo in '70.

PLASTIC FANTASTIC

They included Issey Miyake (*b.*1935), Rei Kawakubo (*b.*1942) under the label Comme des Garçons, Yohji Yamamoto (*b.*1943), Mitsuhiro Matsuda (*b.*1934) and Kenzo (*b.*1940). They all placed enormous importance on texture – Miyake experimented with everything from woven bamboo to moulded plastic – and they used their unusual fabrics to layer, drape and wrap the body.

LIMITED PALETTE

To add emphasis to the texture, designers used a palette of colours that was virtually monochrome, apart from the odd dash of strong colour, such as red.

Exploiting the fashion for eastern chic, Matsuda's collection ('84) was shot in Japan.

A Comme des Garçons jacket ('88) – the year Rei Kawakubo declared that red was 'the new black'.

Some critics condemned the clothes as baggy or shapeless, but the way they combined elements of traditional Japanese costume with modern ideas was completely original.

ANY COLOUR AS LONG AS IT'S WHITE ...

Western designers, too, came up with alternatives to showy power suits. Rifat Ozbek (*b*.1953) showed his new age White collection in '90. The clothes were influenced by clubwear, but most of all their purity expressed a desire to return to simple, clean living.

This Matsuda outfit in rough, cream cottons incorporates a buttoned sling which holds the matching blazer.

ECO-FRIENDLY FASHION

Ironically, environmentally-*un*friendly bleach was used to achieve Ozbek's pristine whites! Katherine Hamnett (*b*.1948), however, had championed the 'green' cause from the mid-'80s. The truly eco-friendly follower of fashion could wear her teeshirts, which were made of cotton that had been grown without the use of pesticides. Often these were printed with slogans stating ecological or political concerns.

Rifat Ozbek took to the cat-walk to greet the applause, surrounded by models wearing his new-age whites ('90). The key to this colourless style was interesting textures.

SUPERMODELS
Despite the supermodels' astronomical fees, using one almost guaranteed front-page coverage in the international press. It could make or break a collection. Such was their success that some supermodels, including Naomi Campbell, Karen Mulder and Claudia Schiffer, even had lookalike dolls launched in '96.

The rise of the supermodel saw cat-walk models such as Caprice Boulet (left), Naomi Campbell (centre) and Claudia Schiffer (right) become international celebrities.

The new ANDROGYNY

Unisex, which had been an influential theme in the 1960s and '70s, continued into the '80s and '90s. Unisex garments included tracksuits, teeshirts, sweatshirts, jeans and leather jackets. Dark colours such as black, grey and khaki were favoured.

Tank Girl (from the '95 movie) dressed in androgynous army gear.

GENDER-BENDERS

As the girls dressed up like boys, some boys went the other way, including pop singers Boy George (who wore make-up and skirts with his long hair plaited and in ribbons) and Marilyn.

Boy George was the most famous gender-bender of the '80s.

WOMEN IN POWER

Even women's power suits, which used elements of masculine dress, could be seen as unisex. But by the early 1990s, the fashion was for androgyny, meaning appearing to be both masculine and feminine.

GIRLS WILL BE BOYS

Men's wardrobes were plundered for inspiration. Screen actresses, such as Marlene Dietrich and Katharine Hepburn had used the trouser suit to great effect in the 1930s and '40s. The trouser suit of the early '90s was made to fit a woman's figure, so that their femininity was not compromised.

In futuristic white make-up for lips, eyes and hair, this model ('84) could be male or female ...

21ST-CENTURY GIRLS

Tank Girl is a comic-strip heroine who lives in the post-apocalyptic 21st century, surviving on her wits and streetwise resilience. The cartoon was made into a feature film in 1995, starring Lori Petty and Malcolm McDowell. Tank Girl's clothes were distressed post-punk, with knee-high combat boots, thick, protective gloves, torn jeans and tight-fitting teeshirts. The overall effect stated a refusal to obey rules of beauty, and was widely imitated.

ON THE CAT-WALK

Many women began to look like men: Jenny Shimuzu, who modelled in Versace's 1994 cat-walk show, challenged stereotypes of beauty with her cropped hair and defined, muscular frame. And Calvin Klein picked up the theme when he launched two fragrances, 'CK One' and 'CK Be,' aimed at both men and women.

Even Chanel put the (very male) tie with her double-breasted cardigan and felt hat for women.

A WOMAN'S TOUCH

Female celebrities who popularized the macho look included the musicians kd lang and Annie Lennox, and actresses Ellen DeGeneres and Sandra Bernhardt. However, it was not just the masculine-styled clothes that were important, but attitude and behaviour.

A tailored women's blazer by Ralph Lauren ('84) and turn-ups suited the gender-bender look.

Margaret Thatcher (b.1925) became Britain's first woman prime minister in '79. She held power for over 11 years.

GIRL *power*

It's hard to believe that until 1979 there had never been a female prime minister or president in Europe. During the '80s, the independent woman became an important image in all media, from advertising to television.

CHANGING VALUES

Magazines such as *Cosmopolitan* recognised that 'getting a man' was no longer a woman's only goal in life. Women wanted careers and financial independence. The VW Golf car advert starring model Paula Hamilton played on this: the scenario was a woman leaving her fiancé and driving off in her car – to a new, independent life.

Madonna's 'Blonde Ambition' tour ('90), saw her in a satin corset with a reinforced bustier, designed by Jean-Paul Gaultier. By the time her daughter was born ('96), Madonna had left behind her raunchy image.

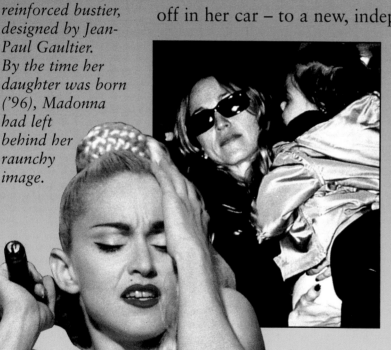

STRONG WOMEN

For young women, pop stars were important role models. Strong, successful singer-songwriters included Annie Lennox and Björk. Neither was afraid to defy convention. Lennox was known for her gender-bending suits, while Björk championed the cause of fresh young designers, including Hussein Chalayan (b.1970). Chalayan created beautiful eveningwear out of Tyvek, a papery material previously used for making envelopes and protective boilersuits!

MATERIAL SUCCESS

Madonna was the biggest pop success of all. From the start, she was unafraid to show naked ambition – or naked bits of body! Her style constantly changed and was widely copied. In the film *Desperately Seeking Susan* she wore big jewellery and tight tube skirts rolled down to reveal her midriff; for the single 'Vogue', her outfit called to mind the slinky eveningwear of 1940s Hollywood. She was also famous for wearing underwear as outerwear, as designed by Gaultier, and even this trickled down to the high street.

LARA CROFT

Lara Croft, heroine of Playstation's *Tomb Raider* game, ran, shot, swam, skied – and looked sexy at the same time! Over her slim figure and large bust she wore revealing, skin-tight clothing. Her only fault was that she was not real!

Lara Croft could be seen as the ideal '90s woman.

SPICE ATTACK

Fans of the Spice Girls could pick and choose from five different looks: Sporty (the latest sports-gear), Baby (baby-doll dresses), Scary (animal-prints), Posh (couture) and Ginger (slinky and daring). The girls launched Girl Power in the mid-1990s, stressing that girls could be loud and have fun: their first hit single revealed "I'll tell you what I want, what I really, really want!"

From left to right: Sporty, Baby, Scary, Posh and Ginger (who left the band in '98).

SUB-cultures

Dance and music has influenced the way people dress throughout the 20th century. The 1950s saw the birth of rock 'n' roll and teenage fans – who copied their idols to the last button or zip. In the '80s and '90s music was again completely revolutionized and that, of course, influenced fashions.

B-BOYS AND FLYGIRLS

Hip-hop and rap were born in New York City's Bronx district. DJs created a new music, in which the chorus was made by 'scratching' records with their bare hands. During these instrumentals (breaks), hangers-on known as b-boys – short for break boys – showed off their break-dancing skills. Although hip-hop started in the mid-1970s, it did not hit the mainstream until the '80s. By then, the girls had a nickname too. They were called flygirls, slang for 'sexy girls'. Both b-boys and flygirls favoured designer sportswear, trainers and chunky gold jewellery, and the boys also shaved their hair into stunning patterns.

Salt-N-Pepa's hit 'Push It' ('87) was one of the first rap tunes to make it in the pop chart. The flygirls' bright, baggy clothes were soon imitated by fans of the music.

DANCE MUSIC

Thanks to hip-hop's irreverence, the record was no longer a sacred object to be played from start to finish. New styles of music developed: techno in Detroit, house in Chicago, then rave in London and Manchester. What was unique about these new sounds was that they were created by mixing together different pieces of music and sound effects. There was no longer a star on the stage for fans to copy. And anyway, they were too busy dancing!

Industrial accessories and fetish fabrics were worn by techno cyberpunks and bands such as the Prodigy.

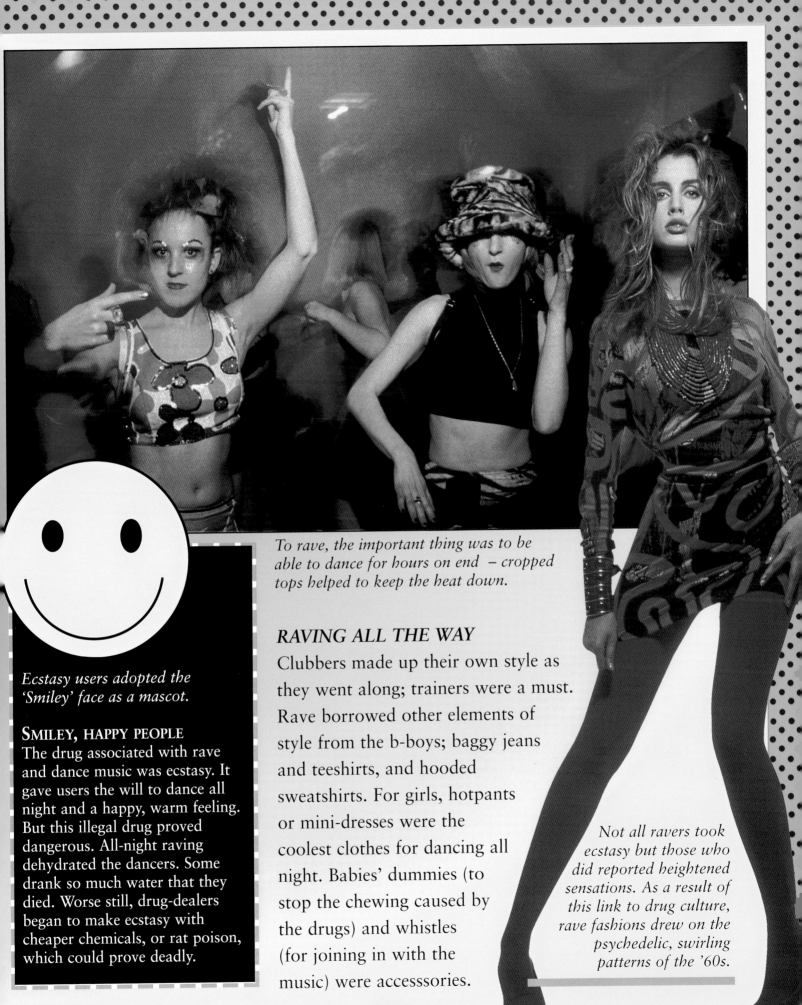

Ecstasy users adopted the 'Smiley' face as a mascot.

SMILEY, HAPPY PEOPLE

The drug associated with rave and dance music was ecstasy. It gave users the will to dance all night and a happy, warm feeling. But this illegal drug proved dangerous. All-night raving dehydrated the dancers. Some drank so much water that they died. Worse still, drug-dealers began to make ecstasy with cheaper chemicals, or rat poison, which could prove deadly.

To rave, the important thing was to be able to dance for hours on end – cropped tops helped to keep the heat down.

RAVING ALL THE WAY

Clubbers made up their own style as they went along; trainers were a must. Rave borrowed other elements of style from the b-boys; baggy jeans and teeshirts, and hooded sweatshirts. For girls, hotpants or mini-dresses were the coolest clothes for dancing all night. Babies' dummies (to stop the chewing caused by the drugs) and whistles (for joining in with the music) were accesssories.

Not all ravers took ecstasy but those who did reported heightened sensations. As a result of this link to drug culture, rave fashions drew on the psychedelic, swirling patterns of the '60s.

SPORTSWEAR
as streetwear

Items such as trainers, tracksuits, cycling shorts and leggings were stretchy and comfortable and began to be worn as casual clothing on the street and in clubs. But you could not wear just any sportswear – the correct label was essential!

STREET CRED

Logos and labels were important for street credibility, whether the latest favourite was Nike, Adidas or Reebok. Boy band New Kids on the Block, for example, wore Nike.

In '86 top hip-hop band Run DMC made the Top 10 with their single 'My Adidas'. They were famous for wearing their trainers unlaced.

Rollerbladers needed protective pads as well as in-line skates.

SPORTS BOOM

Some people did still wear sports clothing to exercise! The fitness fad had started in the '70s, with roller-skating and aerobics. The '80s and '90s saw gyms springing up everywhere, offering the new aerobics craze – step. Outdoor sports fans surfed, rollerbladed, skate- and snowboarded. Nike's line 'Just do it!' summed up the desire to push the body to the limit.

Skateboarding required long, baggy shorts and flat, rubber-soled shoes.

PAYING THE PRICE

The latest high-tech footwear was expensive – way beyond the reach of many youngsters. There were news reports of children and teenagers being mugged for their trainers. An alternative was to buy fake designer trainers, teeshirts, watches or bags. Copies made in the Far East could be on sale within days of a new style appearing in the shops.

Reebok leggings and a vest show off a well-toned physique. Sportswear was easy to wear, so long as the body was in shape.

MARKETING TECHNIQUES

Nike (named after the Greek goddess of victory) had become a household name following the jogging craze of the late 1970s. The company used sports stars to promote its products, including the American basketball player, Michael Jordan, after whom the Air Jordan line of trainers was named. Sportswear brands copied the fashion industry's success by producing new improved designs each season to encourage people to buy the latest model.

Ralph Lauren's Polo range featured cosy sweatshirts with draw-string hoods and drill shorts.

STEALING FROM SPORT

Clothing was borrowed from more rugged sports, too, such as sailing and rock-climbing. Lightweight windcheaters in high-tech Gore-Tex were worn by mountaineers who climbed Mount Everest, but also by ordinary people doing their Saturday shopping. Other modern fibres made their way from the ski slopes, including fleecy Polartec, which was picked up by young, streetwise design labels such as Copperwheat Blundell and Firetrap in the early 1990s and used for snuggly jackets, gloves, scarves and beanie hats. Young people were out to have a good time and wanted to feel warm, comfortable and fashionable.

Haute couture met sportswear in these high-fashion Chanel trainers ('97). The V-neck is by Escada Sport.

GRUNGE

In the early 1990s the grunge look, so-called because it was grungy, dirty and scruffy, became the costume of the student population, as well as student drop-outs. It was a reaction against fashion and, in particular, the radiant image of perfect health that was projected by the supermodels.

Grunge could be a brocade corset with suspenders that held up saggy cotton stockings. Shoes were Doc Martens.

ANTI-FASHION

The recycling of clothes, and past decades and styles became the concern of the young generation, in keeping with environmental issues. Working clothes, such as jeans and flannel shirts were worn with combat boots or ever-popular Doc Martens.

THE GRUNGE SOUND

American pop band Nirvana, from Seattle, in the United States, were as important to the grunge movement as the Sex Pistols had been to punk. They had a multi-platinum album called Nevermind, with tracks called 'Sounds Like Teen Spirit' (which went to No 1) and 'In Bloom'.

Smashed spectacles completed this grungy John Galliano outfit ('85). Unrolled, the sleeves would stretch down to the knees!

GRUNGE GURUS

Nirvana's lead singer Kurt Cobain and his wife, Courtney Love (from the band Hole) were key people in the grunge movement. Love wore short, baby-doll dresses with big combat boots. Her bleached blonde hair was matted and showed dark roots, while the paleness of her skin was highlighted by her dark lipstick. On the cat-walk, waif-like Kate Moss found fame. She had pale skin, a gangly body and lank, tangled hair: along with looking bored, these were all the ingredients for the grunge look!

Girl-band All Saints took the grunge look into the mainstream, wearing combat-style trousers, workmen's boots and old-fashioned anoraks.

DESIGNER GRUNGE

Many upcoming designers rebelled against slick couture. Belgian Martin Margiela (*b.*1957) disregarded usual cat-walk venues and showed his collections in disused warehouses and tube stations. He also famously used what would have been the lining of an outfit as a garment in itself – complete with unfinished seams and tailor tacks!

A New Yorker displayed grungy layering by wearing two jumpers and tying a third round her waist. Her billowing skirt reached down to thick hiking boots.

HEROIN CHIC

Drugs contributed to the deaths of many celebrities. Actor River Phoenix died aged 23 after taking a lethal cocktail of heroin and cocaine in '93. The movie industry was blamed for glamorizing drugs in films such as Quentin Tarantino's *Pulp Fiction* ('94) and Danny Boyle's *Trainspotting* ('96). Some designers exploited the look, which was nicknamed 'heroin chic'. Their models looked very thin, pale and washed out, with dark, hollow eyes.

Drugs caused Kurt Cobain of Nirvana to commit suicide in '94.

RETRO *fashions*

In the final decades of the 20th century, there were many revivals of past styles. It seemed that every fashion had been revisited for inspiration. John Galliano (b.1960), who exploded on to the fashion scene in '84, is well-known for his magpie attitude to fashion. In his collections he has drawn on every possible past style, from frock-coats to kilts to Dior's hour-glass New Look.

Pop star Kid Creole stepped back in time to the '40s in this cream woollen zoot suit ('84).

Chanel shoes and kid gloves ('87) recalled op art of the '60s.

MIX & MATCH MAGPIES

With so many different images appearing in so many different media, there was no longer one single look that was 'in' and individuality counted more than anything. Nevertheless, one era proved most popular for borrowing: the 1970s.

FLARES WITH FLAIR

Just about every designer – from upcoming Alexander McQueen (*b*.1969) to well-established Gucci – showed flares, hipster trousers or pedal-pushers in the '90s. Shoe design, too, took a trip down memory lane as platform soles hit the streets. Vivienne Westwood famously used them in her '93 collection, and Naomi Campbell fell over in them! To add a modern twist, even trainers were given platform soles, as worn by Baby Spice.

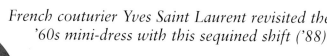
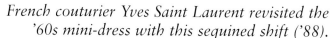

French couturier Yves Saint Laurent revisited the '60s mini-dress with this sequined shift ('88).

BACK TO THE 60s ...

From the 1960s, designers borrowed hotpants (very short shorts), maxi-skirts (of ankle length) and kaftans. Tight, ribbed teeshirts, polo necks, halter necks and tops with a 'keyhole' cut to reveal the cleavage all came back in. Many used '60s-style stripes or psychedelic patterns.

Metallic flares, '90s-style, worn with a silk jacket by Workers for Freedom ('92).

... AND TO THE '50s

The baby-doll look adopted by grunge was based on the nightwear from the late-1950s. Baby-doll pyjamas had consisted of a flouncy vest with matching frilly knickers. The look was picked up by designers Anna Sui (*b.*1955) and Isaac Mizrahi (*b.*1961) for their '94 collections. The general idea was, if a look worked once, it would work again!

New-age travellers owed as much to punk style as to hippie fashions.

Labelled 'new hippies' when they appeared in Vogue *('88), this couple borrowed flower-power style: floppy velvet hats and ethnic beads.*

THE '70s ARE BORN AGAIN

Everyone craved that '70s disco vibe. A musical of *Saturday Night Fever* was a huge success on Broadway and in the West End. At the cinema there was *Boogie Nights* ('98), *Grease* (remastered '98) and a nostalgic film version of the '70s TV hit *The Brady Bunch* ('95).

'70s supergroup ABBA were made popular again with covers by Erasure and tribute band Bjorn Again (below).

The TECHNOLOGY *behind the*

Advances in the chemical industry during the 1980s and '90s created a whole range of exciting new fabrics for designers to work with. State-of-the-art computers were now used to control factory machines and for designing new fabrics. DuPont's wonder fabric Lycra kept on improving and was joined by new synthetics such as Tencel, Polartec and Gore-Tex.

ALL-WEATHER FRIEND

Gore-Tex met the challenge for a waterproof, windproof and 'breathable' fabric suitable for pursuits such as snowboarding. In 1998 Nike brought out Gore-Tex-coated running shoes. And in Autumn '99 Ralph Lauren's brand-new label RLX introduced Gore-Tex in its ski, cross-training, snowboard and cycling collections.

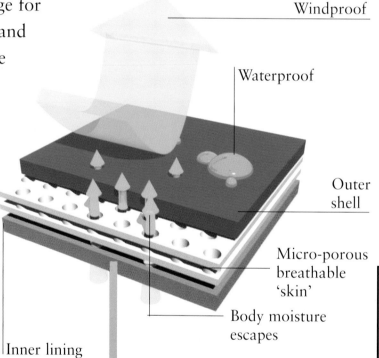

Windproof

Waterproof

Outer shell

Micro-porous breathable 'skin'

Body moisture escapes

Inner lining

With its fantastic qualities of keeping out the elements while letting perspiration evaporate, Gore-Tex is a perfect fabric for outdoor sports.

Gore-Tex's waterproof 'skin' contains nearly 1.4 billion pores per sq cm. Each pore is 20,000 times smaller than a raindrop, but 700 times bigger than a molecule of water vapour, such as perspiration.

As technologies improve, textile manufacturers are able to experiment by bonding different fibres. Here natural silk is combined with synthetic nylon.

fashions of the 80s & 90s

A computer controls the production line at an ICI textile plant. Designers even use computers to work out their new collections on-screen.

French designer Myrlold picked up on the 'green' vogue for recycling by transforming plastic bags into amazing dresses and coats.

GOING 'GREEN'

Green concerns led manufacturers to develop new, eco-friendly fabrics. Polartec, a thermal fleece, was made from recycled plastic bottles. Tencel, a strong, stretchy fabric, was made from renewable wood pulp and was used by designers Calvin Klein and Donna Karan in their collections.

Natural rubber made a comeback in the '80s and '90s. This dress was worn with a clear plastic belt designed by Jean-Paul Gaultier.

BEYOND THE YEAR 2000

As the fashion industry moves into the 21st century, new technologies provide ever-more amazing fabrics. Young designers such as Deborah Milner and Errol Peak are already creating space-age metallic clothes made from polyester-coated stainless steel and aluminium yarns. Sci-fi predictions for 21st-century fashions are becoming science fact.

GLOSSARY

ANDROGYNOUS Showing both male and female traits, for example when a man looks like a woman.

BROCADE A rich, elaborate fabric with a raised design woven into it, often in silk, gold or silver threads.

BRODERIE ANGLAISE A technique used to decorate cotton and linen by making patterns with holes and stitches.

BUSTIER A kind of corset that reaches only to the waist and which includes a bra. Originally underwear, bustiers became popular as outerwear in the '80s and early '90s.

CAPITALISM An economic system based on private (rather than state) ownership of businesses, factories, transport services and so on.

DOC MARTENS Leather boots with laces and thick soles, which were part of skinhead 'uniform' in the '60s.

FISHNET A large, open weave knit often used for stockings and tights.

GORE-TEX A synthetic fabric which is windproof and waterproof, but which also lets the wearer's skin 'breathe'.

HOTPANTS Very brief shorts first worn in the late '60s and early '70s.

KNICKERBOCKERS Baggy trousers which fasten just below the knee.

NEW LOOK A style of dress made popular by Christian Dior in 1947. Dresses had fitted bodices, tiny waists and very full skirts.

POLARTEC A fleece-like synthetic fabric with excellent thermal (heat-retaining) properties. It is made from recycled plastic bottles.

RA-RA SKIRT A very short frilly skirt originally worn by American cheerleaders.

TENCEL A strong, stretchy, artificial fabric made from wood pulp.

UNISEX Clothes designed to be worn by either sex; they first became popular in the '60s.

YUPPIE Short for 'young, upwardly-mobile professional'; used to describe an ambitious young man or woman who is pursuing a professional career.

TIMELINE

	WORLD EVENTS	TECHNOLOGY	FAMOUS PEOPLE	ART & MEDIA
0	•*Start of Iran-Iraq war* •*Poland: Solidarity set up*	•*Transformer toys go on market*	•*John Lennon shot*	•*Anthony Burgess:* Earthly Powers
1		•*First space shuttle,* Columbia, *launched*	•*Prince Charles and Lady Diana marry*	•The Face *launched*
2	•*Falklands War: Britain defeats Argentina*	•*First artificial heart is transplanted*	•*Death of Princess Grace of Monaco*	•*Ridley Scott:* Blade Runner
3	•*US & Caribbean troops invade Grenada*	•*CDs first go on sale* •*AIDS virus isolated*	•*Lech Walesa awarded Nobel Peace Prize*	•*First episode of* Dynasty
4	•*New Zealand declared a nuclear-free zone*	•*Apple Macintosh launched*	•*Bob Geldorf sets up Bandaid pop charity*	•*Madonna: 'Like a Virgin'*
5	•*USSR: Gorbachev becomes leader*	•*Tele-shopping in USA* •*Sinclair's 3-wheel C-5*		•*Norman Foster: Hong Kong & Shanghai Bank*
6	•*Chernobyl nuclear disaster*	•*Space shuttle* Challenger *explodes*	•*Cory Aquino wins Philippines election*	•*Richard Rogers: Lloyds Building*
7	•*Black Friday stock market crash*		•*Terry Waite taken hostage in Beirut*	•*Toni Morrison:* Beloved
8	•*End of Iran-Iraq war* •*Lockerbie air disaster*	•*Stephen Hawking: A* Brief History of Time	•*Benazir Bhutto prime minister of Pakistan*	
9	•*China: Tiananmen Square massacre*	•*Nintendo launch Game Boy video game*	•*Ayatollah Khomeini dies*	•*Chadwick:* Enfleshings •*Batman*
0	•*Gulf War breaks out as Iraq invades Kuwait*	•*Launch of Hubble Space Telescope*	•*Nelson Mandela freed in South Africa*	•*Philippe Starck: Juicy Salif*
1	•*Break-up of USSR* •*Yeltzin is Russian leader*	•*Dyson's bagless vacuum cleaner wins design prize*	•*Aung San Suu Kyi wins Nobel Peace Prize*	•*Pat Barker:* Regeneration
2	•*Australia drops oath of loyalty to Queen*			•*Frank Gehry: 'Powerplay' armchair*
3	•*PLO & Israel sign peace agreement*		•*Bill Clinton becomes US president*	•*Stephen Spielberg:* Jurassic Park
4	•*S. Africa: Mandela is first black president*	•*Channel Tunnel completed*	•*Kurt Cobain commits suicide*	•*Tarantino:* Pulp Fiction
5	•*USA: terrorist bomb blast in Oklahoma City*		•*O.J. Simpson acquitted in murder trial*	•*Lori Petty in* Tank Girl
6	•*'Mad Cow' disease: bans on British beef*	•*Sony Playstation is launched*		•*Disney:* Toy Story
7		•*IBM's* Deep Blue *beats Kasparov at chess*	•*Death of Diana, Princess of Wales*	•*Jurassic Park: The Lost World*
8		•*International Space Station:construction begins*		
9	•*Serbians drive Albanians from Kosovo*		•*Madonna is face of Max Factor*	•*Lucas:* Episode 1 The Phantom Menace

INDEX